Living in a Desert

Contents   **Page**

written by Pam Holden

1

A desert is a big, dry place that doesn't get much rain. It is a hard place to live, because everything needs water.

The cactus is a desert plant that keeps water inside. Other plants grow long roots to get water from under the ground.

Small animals that live in hot deserts
are rats, snakes, insects, and lizards.
They hide under rocks or the sand to
keep out of the sun in the daytime.

At night, when it gets cold, they come out to find food and water.

Desert birds like to get away from the heat, too. Some fly high in the sky all day. Other birds only come out at night to find water and to eat insects and seeds.

Ostriches live in the deserts in Africa. They are the biggest birds in the world. They are taller than people! Ostriches can't fly, but they can run fast across the hot desert.

Camels are large animals that can walk for many days with no food or water. Then they drink a lot of water at one time. They have humps on their backs to store fat for food.

People ride camels across the desert, or they use them to take heavy loads.

Not many people live in deserts
because it's hard to find water.
Some people live in huts or tents.

10

They have sheep and goats to get wool and meat and milk. They take their animals across the desert to find food.

11

An oasis is a green place in the middle of a desert. Trees and grass and plants grow there because it has some water.

People can grow vegetables and palm trees for food. They build their houses with bricks made of mud.

Deserts can be windy places sometimes.
The sand blows around in sandstorms.

People need clothes that are long and loose because of the sun and wind and sand. They need warm clothes at night.

Living in a desert is a hard life for plants and animals and people.